mac 2003

Cartoons from the *Daily Mail*

Stan McMurtry **mac**
Edited by Mark Bryant

ROBSON BOOKS

For my dear friend Singie

First published in Great Britain in 2003 by Robson Books,
The Chrysalis Building, Bramley Road, London W10 6SP

An imprint of Chrysalis Books Group plc

Copyright © 2003 Stan McMurtry

Selection and text copyright © 2003 Mark Bryant

British Library Cataloguing in Publication Data
A catalogue record for this title is available from the British Library

ISBN 1 86105 677 X

Typeset by SX Composing DTP, Rayleigh, Essex
Printed in Great Britain by St Edmundsbury Press,
Bury St Edmunds, Suffolk

As the countdown to war with Iraq began, a report from the Agriculture and Environment Biotechnology Commission revealed that research was under way to produce genetically modified livestock, including pigs and poultry that feel no pain.

'If you could delay things a little longer, Prime Minister. Some of the troops aren't quite ready . . .' *5 September 2002*

Nearly half a million protesters organised by the Countryside Alliance marched on London to voice their opposition to Labour's policies on rural Britain which threatened their livelihoods.

'They promised they'd be back early. I bet they're in some seedy London pub.' *23 September*

The Government pledged to ban fox-hunting with dogs. Meanwhile, Tony Blair presented to Parliament a 50-page 'dossier of death' detailing Saddam Hussein's arsenal of weapons of mass destruction, some allegedly deployable at 45 minutes' notice.

'Are you sure this is wise, Divine One? If Blair finds out you like fox-hunting he's bound to attack.' *24 September*

The Royal Family's involvement with politics was questioned when it was revealed that Prince Charles had sent a number of secret letters to the Lord Chancellor, Lord Irvine, complaining about the growth of a US-style 'compensation culture' in Britain.

'I do wish he wouldn't leave Milk Tray every time he delivers a note.' *26 September*

The publication of the diaries of former Tory Health Minister Edwina Currie revealed that she had had a four-year affair with cricket-loving future Prime Minister John Major when she was a backbencher in the 1980s.

'John, have you seen today's papers?' *30 September*

As the tension over Iraq's alleged possession of weapons of mass destruction grew, the United Nations demanded access to all areas of the country including Saddam Hussein's presidential palace compounds, hitherto closed to UN weapons inspectors.

'A headache? What's the matter with you? You've always got headaches nowadays!' *3 October*

A report in the *New Scientist* revealed that bedbugs, thought to have been eradicated by DDT in the 1960s, had reappeared in Britain. The huge rise in infestation was blamed on furniture bought at car boot sales and increased foreign travel.

'What d'you mean, "You were wonderful, darling"? – I'm in here.' *4 October*

Disgraced novelist and former MP Jeffrey Archer prompted a Home Office inquiry after his diaries criticising life in jail were published while he was still serving four years for perjury in Lincoln Prison.

' "Wednesday: Disgusting stew again for lunch, surrounded as usual by fat, moronic thugs with halitosis and not a brain between them . . ." ' *7 October*

One of the proposals made at the Conservative Party conference in Bournemouth was to expand the 'right to buy' scheme for council tenants, introduced in the 1980s, to include the million or so people who currently live in housing-association properties.

'Fantastic news. If the Tories get in we can buy this place.'   *10 October*

A Japanese company announced that it had developed a translation system called Bow-Lingual which it claimed could convert the barks, howls and whines of dogs into human language.

'You heard me. You've got ten minutes. If you're not back from the pub and opening a can of Doggydins by then the cat goes in the microwave!' *11 October*

There was a public outcry when National Lottery money was once again granted to a number of causes that seemed to be unworthy, including £200,000 given to a group which had helped reinstate pupils who had been expelled for issuing death-threats to teachers.

'Wake up, Donald. Another Lottery grant has arrived!' *15 October*

In an attempt to cut road deaths, particularly those involving children, Transport Secretary Alistair Darling announced plans to introduce speed humps and reduce speed limits to 20 mph across wide areas of towns and cities, especially near schools.

'I'm not parked. I'm moving!' *18 October*

More details of the private life of Angus Deayton – presenter of BBC TV's *Have I Got News For You* satirical quiz show – were published, including the revelation that he had had an affair with a woman while on holiday with his pregnant partner.

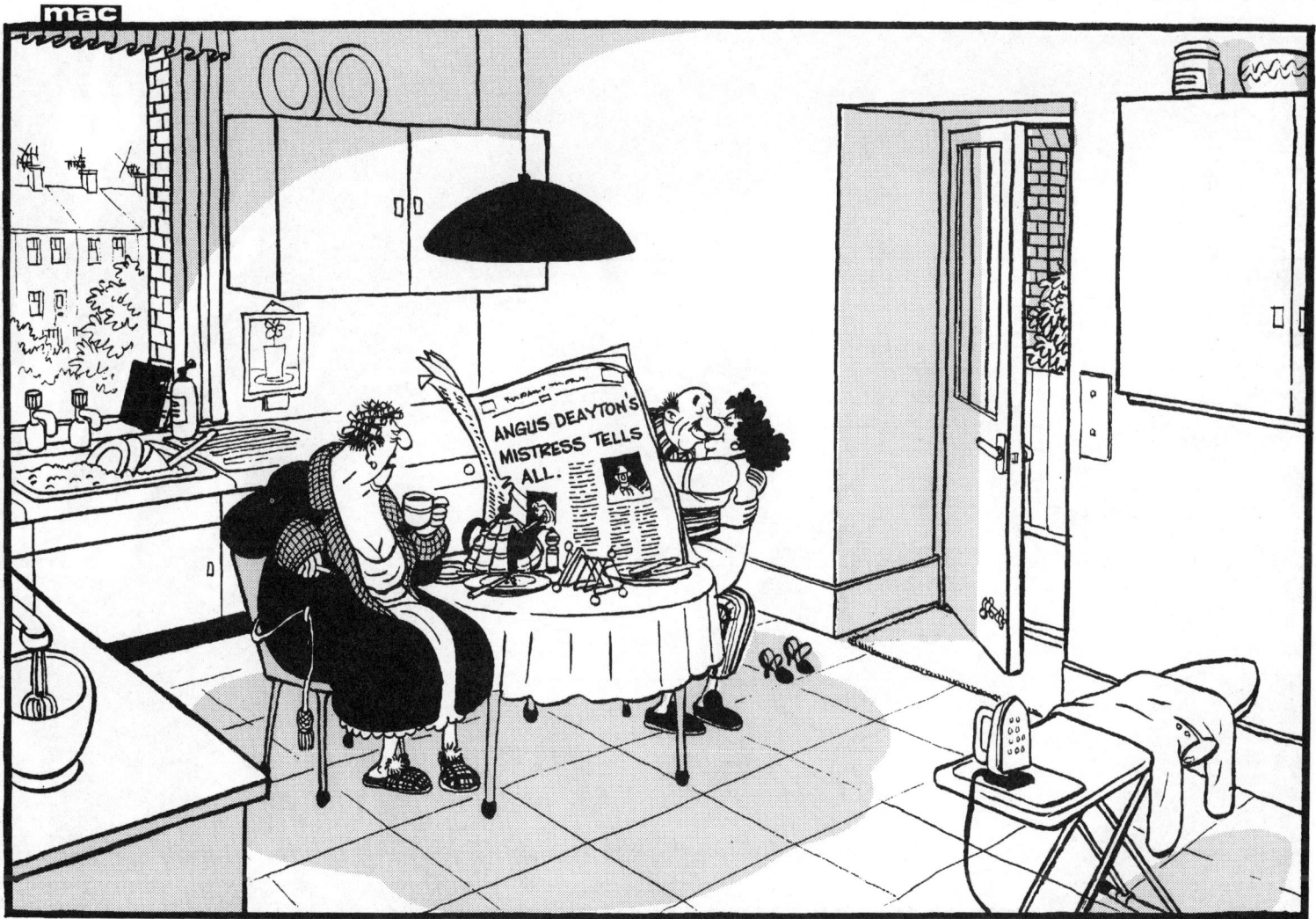

'The part I find hard to believe is that all this happened right under his wife's nose.' *21 October*

The spectre of a new 'Winter of Discontent' loomed as the crisis over the proposed firemen's strike over pay deepened and other unions threatened mass walkouts and sympathy action.

'Never mind about preparing yourself mentally for the big day – you're not on strike till next week!' *22 October*

Ulrika Jonsson published her autobiography, *Honest*, in which she claimed to have been date-raped by a famous TV presenter, later named as *Blue Peter*'s John Leslie, while working as a trainee TV weather girl in the 1980s.

'Damn! Missed it again. I do wish he'd let her finish the weather forecast occasionally.' *24 October*

As a result of watching US TV serials, British children increasingly adopted the US custom of 'trick or treat' on Halloween night. Meanwhile, Angus Deayton was finally axed from the BBC after further revelations about his drug-taking and sex life.

'What did you get at Angus Deayton's place, trick or treat?' *31 October*

After a 24-hour police surveillance operation to catch youths who vandalised brakes on 22 cars parked in Epsom, Surrey, the culprits were discovered to be foxes who had become addicted to the sweet taste of brake fluid and gnawed through the pipes.

'You can always tell when they've been on the brake fluid.' *1 November*

The 21-month trial of Princess Diana's former butler – accused of stealing more than 300 of her personal items – collapsed when the Queen recalled that she had allowed him to hold some of Diana's possessions 'for safe keeping' after her death.

'Dear Ma'am. I wonder if you remember our little chat outside Lloyds Bank last year when I told you I was takin' £250,000 in used fivers 'ome for safe-keepin' . . . ?' *4 November*

David Beckham, multi-millionaire captain of the England football team, increased security at his mansion in Sawbridgeworth, Hertfordshire, after police foiled an alleged plot to kidnap his wife, Victoria, and two young sons, Romeo and Brooklyn.

'Victoria, it's me, David. Can you remember the combination? I want to come in and give you all a goodnight kiss . . .'

5 November

Following the collapse of the trial of Princess Diana's butler, Paul Burrell, a number of revelations about life at Kensington Palace were published, including the allegation that Diana's lovers had sometimes been smuggled in by hiding in the boot of her car.

'I'm sorry, m'lady. I've been out all night and it's all I could find.' *7 November*

As war with Iraq drew ever closer, Britain was put on full alert for a possible attack by Al-Qaeda terrorists. Meanwhile, Buckingham Palace was rocked by claims that a former valet of Prince Charles had been raped by another male royal servant.

'Oh dear. I wonder where they'll strike first?'   *12 November*

Ancient 'Green Goddess' fire-tenders operated by troops were called in when members of the Fire Brigades Union went on strike after rejecting a 'derisory and insulting' Government pay offer of 11% in reply to their demand for a 40% rise in salary.

'I can't do it. It's too embarrassing – *you* ring for a Green Goddess.'   *14 November*

In the biggest shake-up in alcohol licensing laws for 90 years the Government revealed plans to allow Britain's pubs to open 24 hours a day.

'Another half pint? Don't be silly. I've got to drive home for breakfast in a couple of hours' time.' *15 November*

Buckingham Palace announced that it had appointed Sir Michael Peat, the Prince of Wales's chief courtier, to head an investigation into claims that a number of royal servants had plundered memorabilia worth millions of pounds from the Royal Family.

'A Chippendale table, ma'am? Are you sure? I don't remember a table being there.' *18 November*

Crowds of fans gathered outside the Hotel Adlon in Berlin were horrified when pop star Michael Jackson, renowned for plastic surgery to his nose, dangled his new baby over the balcony of his fourth-floor suite, 50 feet above street level.

'Just thought you ought to know, Michael. The baby's dangling your plastic nose over the balcony.' *21 November*

Princess Anne became the first member of the Royal Family since Charles I to gain a criminal record when she was fined £500 under the Dangerous Dogs Act after one of her English bull-terriers bit two boys riding their bikes in Windsor Great Park.

'Having to appear in court . . . a £500 fine. Boy, I've never seen her so cross.' *22 November*

Contestants for the controversial Miss World competition, due to be held in Abuja, Nigeria, had to be flown to London after riots by Muslim extremists led to more than 200 deaths.

'Whooooar! It's hard to believe those gorgeous, pouting girls with their tempting, voluptuous bodies could provoke all that violence.' *25 November*

According to the medical journal *Headache*, a clinical trial involving 160 patients at the Women's Headache Centre in Turin, Italy, found that women who received acupuncture had fewer migraines and needed less medication to prevent headaches.

'Another headache? Er, don't worry, dear. I'm a bit tired anyway.' *26 November*

Before the Sangatte refugee centre near Calais closed, the Government agreed to accept half of its 1,800 asylum-seekers. Meanwhile, Chancellor Gordon Brown announced that he would borrow £100 billion to finance public-sector spending plans.

'Come on in. You'll be all right. We've just borrowed £100 billion.' *29 November*

There was a public outcry when it was revealed that the boyfriend of Cherie Blair's 'lifestyle guru' Carole Caplin had negotiated a huge discount on the price of two flats in Bristol on behalf of the Prime Minister and his wife.

'Mr Blair's agent asks if we'll knock £20,000 off the price, dear. I think that's a jolly good offer, don't you?' *2 December*

As Saddam Hussein handed over a 12,000-page dossier to the United Nations, detailing his chemical and biological weapons programmes, it was reported that Carole Caplin had 'scrubbed the toxins out of Mrs Blair's body' while both were naked in a shower.

'With respect, Mr President, concentrating on Saddam's dossier is difficult enough without you keep saying: "Wowee, ain't that Cherie Blair broad somethin'!"' *9 December*

In an unprecedented move, Cherie Blair made a public statement about the Bristol flats sale scandal, which had been highlighted by the *Daily Mail*. Meanwhile, the Government announced plans for new road-building and motorway-widening schemes.

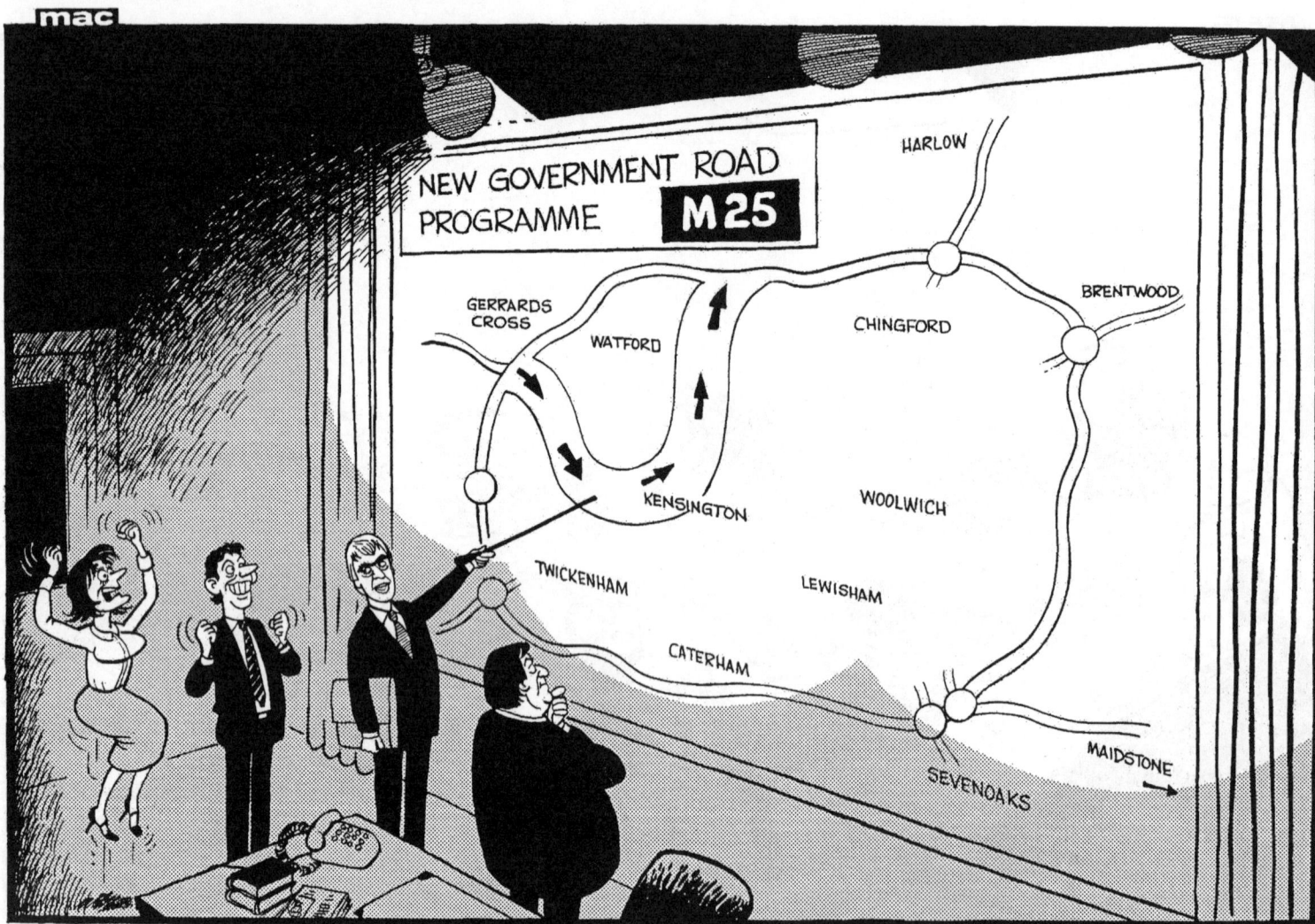

'This one's for you, Cherie. The new ten-lane M25 slip-road goes right through the *Daily Mail* building.'   *12 December*

A Dutch engineering company unveiled a new 'flying car' which will be available in 2006. The £50,000 two-seater, three-wheeled Autocopter has a top speed of 110 mph and can refuel at ordinary petrol stations.

'You and your big mouth! – "Ho, ho. A three-wheeler, my you have come down in the world." '   *13 December*

In an attempt to cut alcohol-related deaths over the festive season, the charity Crimestoppers set up a confidential hotline offering a £500 reward to anyone who reported suspected drink-drivers.

'Time, ladies and gentlemen. Your cars await you. Foot hard down. Last one home's a ninny.' *16 December*

Work and Pensions Secretary Andrew Smith announced plans to scrap the official retirement age of 65, allowing men and women to work on into their 70s and beyond.

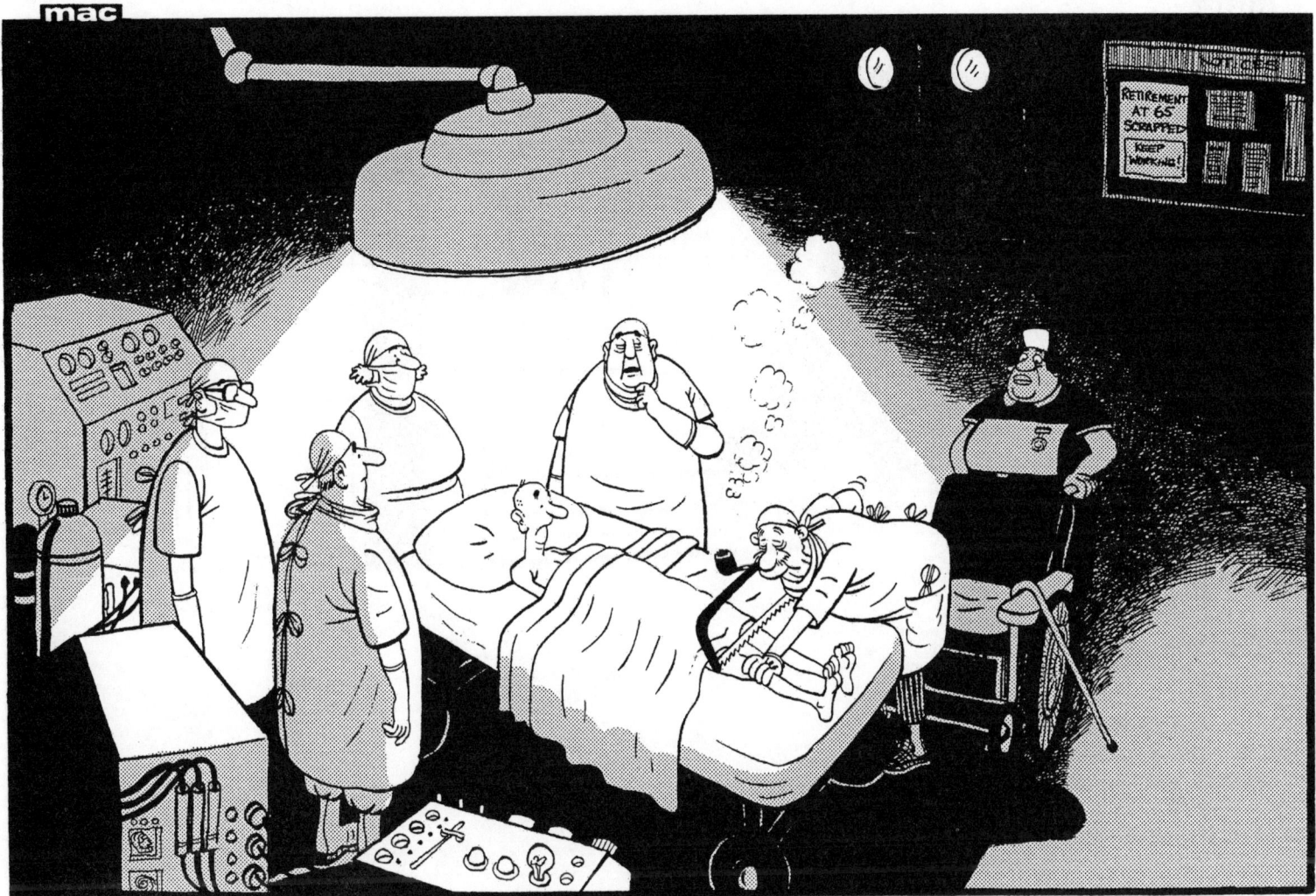

'Hang on, Chief Surgeon. A little senior moment here. Lobotomies are done at the other end, remember?' *17 December*

The Californian film producer Steve Bing set up a trust fund worth £1.8 million for the son he fathered with Liz Hurley, despite statements from the actress and former Estée Lauder model that she would refuse any payments from her estranged lover.

Translation: 'Ignore her, Dad. She's gone bonkers! We're talking pensions here. I don't want to work past 65!' *19 December*

Transport Secretary Alistair Darling announced that armed 'sky marshals' would fly undercover on British passenger jets amid growing fears of a terrorist attack.

ARMED GUARDS FOR BRITISH AIRLINES

'Things must be worse than we thought!' *20 December*

As the tension over the situation in Iraq increased, President Saddam Hussein was accused of playing hide-and-seek with UN inspectors who had still failed to find any evidence of chemical or biological weapons.

'Here they come now. Don't forget, this is Santa's factory and you are his little elves.' *23 December*

To protect endangered cod stocks, new EU directives were introduced to limit Britain's North Sea fishing fleet, reducing the time that trawlers were allowed out of port from 15 to nine days each month.

'It's worth a try, but I still don't think anyone's going to mistake us for cod.' *24 December*

In an effort to cope with the massive immigration crisis, the Government announced that some of Britain's country houses and hotels would be pressed into service as temporary 'induction centres' to accommodate those claiming asylum.

'From what I can gather, m'lord, they want to know if they can borrow the Rolls to go and pick up their benefits.'

21 January 2003

Tony Blair faced the biggest backbench revolt since he came to power when it was announced that universities would be allowed to charge 'top-up fees' for students, leaving graduates with potential debts of up to £21,000 each.

'. . . So by tomorrow, then. A thousand words on: "Will top-up fees have a detrimental effect on university education?" '

23 January

The manufacturers of Tupperware plastic containers announced that 'Tupperware Parties' – a feature of suburban life for more than 40 years – were to be axed in the UK, claiming that British consumers no longer wished to buy its product in this way.

'I'm going to enjoy breaking this news. – No more Tupperware parties!' *24 January*

A 57-year-old British Airways pilot faced the sack after failing a breath test at Arlanda Airport, Stockholm, minutes before he was due to fly a passenger jet to London.

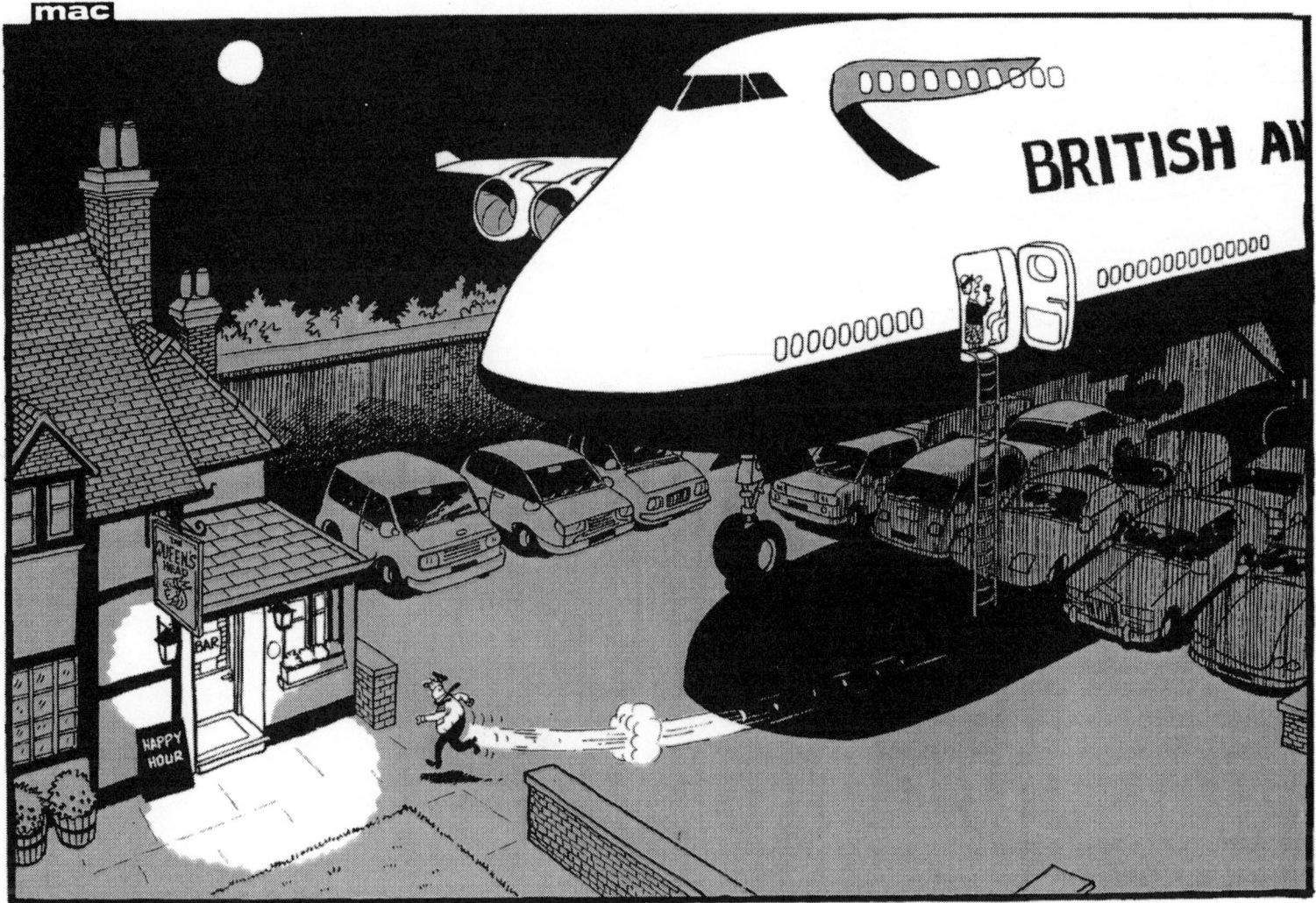

'British Airways apologises for the unscheduled stop. This is for urgent refuelling purposes . . .' *27 January*

In his official report the UN's chief arms inspector, Dr Hans Blix, said that he and his team had failed to find any weapons of mass destruction in Iraq. Meanwhile, the threat of war sent the stock market into a nose dive and share prices tumbled.

'Come on, keep looking. The sooner we can find these weapons of mass destruction for Hans Blix, the sooner my shares will go up again.' *28 January*

New EU animal-welfare regulations introduced from Brussels stipulated that pigs must be given 'environment enrichment' in the form of toys such as footballs or hanging chains. British farmers faced fines of up £1,000 if they failed to comply.

'Well, honestly! I'd just changed Barbie's dress and tucked her up in her little cot, then you go and do that on her!'   *30 January*

In the biggest shake-up of the sex laws for 50 years, Home Secretary David Blunkett introduced a new Sexual Offences Bill which made it illegal to have sex in public. Meanwhile, blizzards brought London and the south-east to a standstill.

'They're lucky. If the temperature hadn't dropped suddenly they'd be facing a jail sentence.' *31 January*

In a unique ITV documentary about his life, millionaire pop star Michael Jackson spoke of his plastic surgery treatment and also revealed that in a single shopping spree in Las Vegas he had once spent nearly £6 million on household goods.

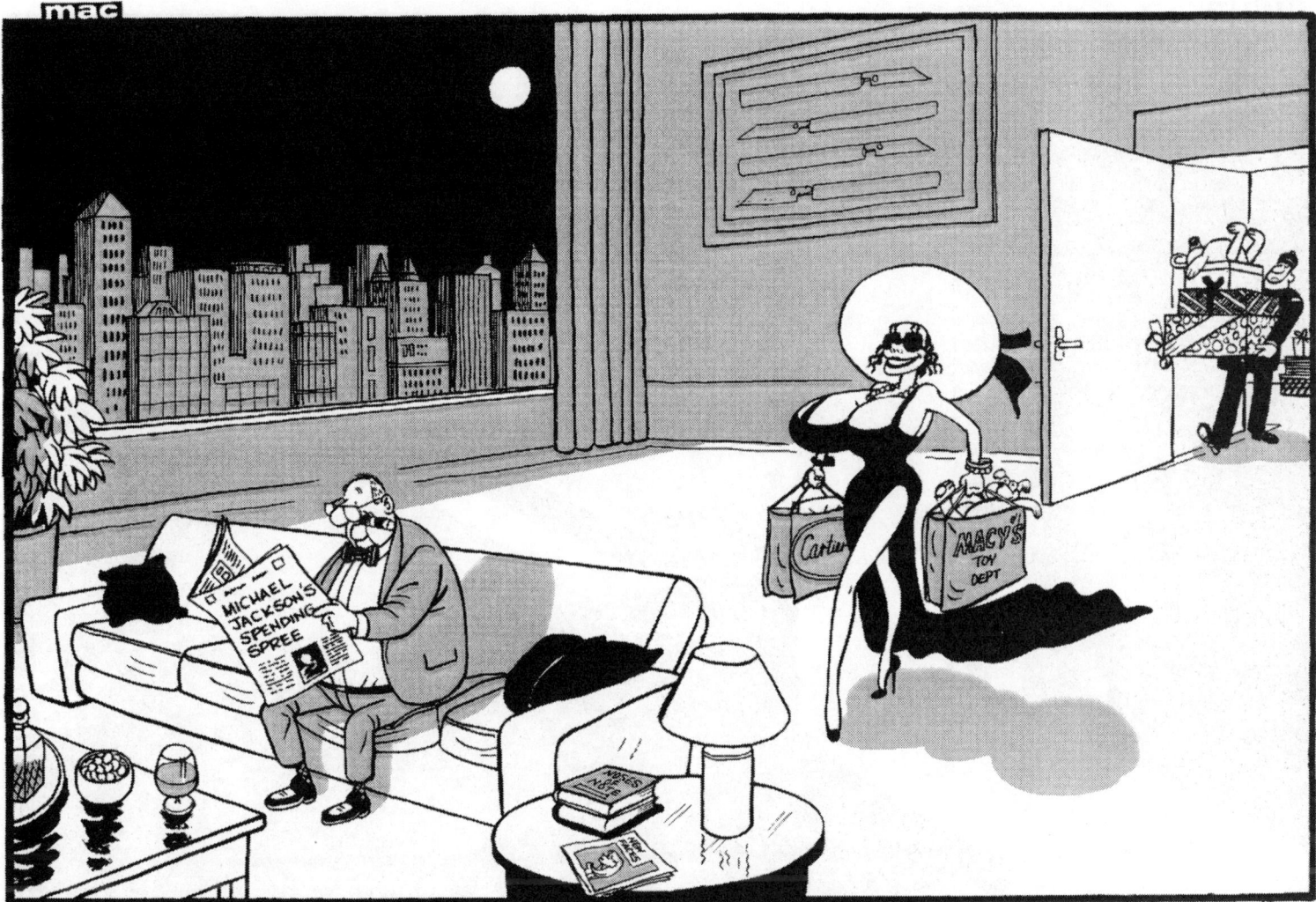

'Five and a half million bucks? Wow, Michael! What did you spend it on?' *3 February*

A 57-year-old grandmother from Surrey became Britain's second-oldest mother when she gave birth after receiving IVF treatment.

'Cooee, lover man. I know you're there. I can hear your knees knocking.' *4 February*

Deputy Prime Minister John Prescott unveiled a £22-billion plan to build another 200,000 homes in the south-east of England by 2016, leading to fears that even more areas of countryside would be swallowed up.

'This used to be the long par five.' *6 February*

Belfast-born Andre Stitt, a 44-year-old 'performance creator', received a £12,000 community arts grant to stage a number of shows, including 'White Trash Curry Kick', in which he kicked an empty curry carton through Bedford town centre.

'This new work of art you bought me – when can it be hung?'   *7 February*

Lord Irvine, the millionaire Lord Chancellor – who had been criticised in 1998 over the huge cost of the wallpaper used to refurbish his official residence – hit the headlines again when he was forced to decline a bumper 12.6% (£22,700) pay rise.

'You idiot! We could have bought that last roll of wallpaper we need!' *10 February*

NATO faced a crisis when deep divisions appeared among its members over the situation in Iraq, with Russia opposing the military action proposed by the USA and Britain and backing instead a new peace-plan put forward by France and Germany.

'Hush, gentlemen. I want to see how the war is going between America and her allies.' *11 February*

After intelligence reports suggested that Al-Qaeda terrorists were planning to shoot down a passenger jet, hundreds of troops accompanied by Scimitar tanks were sent to patrol Heathrow Airport.

'They're on to us, I tell you! It's about that extra bottle of whisky in your hand-luggage.' *13 February*

On St Valentine's Day, armed police joined soldiers deployed at airports nationwide in the search for shoulder-launched missiles and other anti-aircraft weapons suspected of being used by terrorists.

'Honestly – I was going to fire a plastic arrow with a rose on it through our bedroom window!' *14 February*

Prime Minister Tony Blair's leadership seemed to be in jeopardy as a million peace protesters marched through London to demonstrate against Britain going to war with Iraq, and many senior members of the Labour Party threatened to resign.

'OK, everybody. Keep in line!'   *17 February*

Football star David Beckham was cut in the face when Manchester United's manager, Sir Alex Ferguson, kicked a football boot at him in the dressing-room following the team's defeat by Arsenal in the FA Cup.

'Second half and here come Manchester United, no doubt refreshed by half an orange each and a pep-talk from their manager . . .' *18 February*

New rules introduced by Home Secretary David Blunkett to curb bogus asylum-seekers, by denying benefits to those who fail to claim asylum as soon as they enter Britain, were declared illegal by the High Court.

'Sometimes, Sadie, I feel you're the only one I can trust – you wouldn't be letting in every down-on-their-luck asylum-seeker . . .'

20 February

A tribunal judging a claim for constructive unfair dismissal against Plymouth Hospitals NHS Trust heard that an orthopaedic surgeon had been asked to use an ordinary dessert spoon in a hip operation rather than an approved surgical curette.

'You're lucky. Last week we had to manage with just a dessert spoon.' *21 February*

Defence Secretary Geoff Hoon was criticised for taking his family skiing in the French Alps at a time when 40,000 British troops were preparing to go to war with Iraq amid complaints of inadequate supplies, including a shortage of toilet paper.

'Stirring news, men. At great risk to himself, and to help us here in the Gulf, our Defence Secretary has single-handedly stolen two toilet rolls from his hotel in the French Alps . . .' *24 February*

Geoff Hoon, who reportedly had not had a break from work since Christmas, returned from holiday to inspect British troops stationed in Kuwait in the final build-up for the invasion of Iraq.

'Oh, stop moaning! I haven't had a break since Christmas either.' *25 February*

After at first refusing to carry out Dr Hans Blix's order to destroy Saddam Hussein's banned Al-Samoud II missiles, the Iraqis eventually began to dismantle them.

'There, what did I tell you? It's not our job. The army should dismantle them.' *3 March*

Residents in Luton, Bedfordshire, were furious when it was discovered that young asylum-seekers aged six to 17 were to receive free golf lessons from professional coaches at the local Kevin Duggan Junior Golf Academy.

'Just a little tip on etiquette here. Try saying: "Good shot, old chap. Drinks on me at the nineteenth." ' *4 March*

The Headmasters' and Headmistresses' Conference joined forces with the Girls' Schools Association to boycott Bristol University when it announced a controversial campaign to reject top-grade applicants in favour of those from 'disadvantaged backgrounds'.

'It's true, darling. I caught him red-handed – swotting! Now he'll never get to university.' *6 March*

France, Russia and Germany joined forces to oppose British and US plans to attack Iraq.
Meanwhile, the trial began of a man accused of cheating on ITV's *Who Wants To Be a Millionaire?*
quiz by listening to coughs from an accomplice in the audience.

7 March

Splits appeared in the Cabinet over the prospect of Britain and the USA attacking Iraq without UN backing. International Development Secretary Clare Short threatened to resign over the issue and accused the Prime Minister of being 'reckless'.

'Right. Hands up those who think the nasty man should be given a smacked bottom so everyone else can live happily ever after . . . Good, that's fairly conclusive. The ayes have it.' *10 March*

Former Welsh Secretary Ron Davies, who had lost his Cabinet post after a gay sex encounter in London in 1998, resigned from the Welsh Assembly after being spotted near a notorious gay haunt off the M4. He claimed he had been looking for badgers.

'I had to let them in. Ron Davies is out there looking for badgers.' *11 March*

In a blitz on Britain's 'yob culture', Home Secretary David Blunkett extended the power to hand out on-the-spot fines for anti-social behaviour to include park wardens and shopping-centre security guards as well as police and community-support officers.

'Blunkett's scheme is working, Sarge. I've fined someone for yobbish behaviour – he's getting the money now.' *13 March*

As Prince Charles visited Bulgaria and received more official presents, the Peat Report into the sale of royal gifts by members of his staff was published.

'I believe one of the servants sold it while you were in Bulgaria, sir.'   *14 March*

Hard on the heels of the Peat Report into the royal 'gifts for cash' scandal, it was revealed that Princess Diana had recorded a number of video tapes in which she talked frankly about intimate details of her life with Prince Charles.

'Will you tell him or shall I? William is on a mugging charge and Harry's joined Al-Qaeda.' *17 March*

Tony Blair returned to face a rebellious House of Commons after attending a summit in the Azores at which the US president, George W Bush, declared that a 'moment of truth' had arrived over the war with Iraq.

'It's the Prime Minister's moment of truth – you have to admire his bravery.' *18 March*

As the war on Iraq began with a massive aerial bombardment, the Home Office advised British householders to prepare for possible terrorist counter-attacks by stocking up on torches, blankets, bottled water and canned food.

'Don't come out yet, Mavis. Here he comes again – GET BACK, SADDAM, YOU SWINE! WHAT'S IN THAT CANISTER? . . . OH MY GOD! . . . OUCH! TAKE THAT . . . AND THAT!' *20 March*

The appearance of Saddam Hussein on Iraqi TV cast doubts on US claims that he had been killed or seriously injured – but was it really the president or just one of his many doubles? Meanwhile, the 75th Academy Awards ceremony was held in Hollywood.

'Wonderful news, Divine One. I got an Oscar for all my impersonations of you.' *24 March*

The war in Iraq was the first 'media war' in which there was non-stop live TV coverage by broadcasters on both sides of the conflict.

'War, war, war! Is anything else on the other channel?'   *25 March*

A survey conducted by the National Association of Schoolmasters and the Union of Women Teachers reported almost 1,000 incidents of verbal or physical abuse of staff by pupils at 300 schools over a two-week period.

'I'm warning you, Potter. If you don't stop your bullying, I'm going to tell my Mummy – and my Mummy's bigger than your Mummy!' *27 March*

As the mystery of the whereabouts of Saddam Hussein and his powerful second son, Qusay, deepened, it was revealed that the Iraqi president had already smuggled the rest of his family out of the country before the bombing started.

'We made it, Qusay – Syria!' *28 March*

Britain celebrated Mothering Sunday on 30 March.

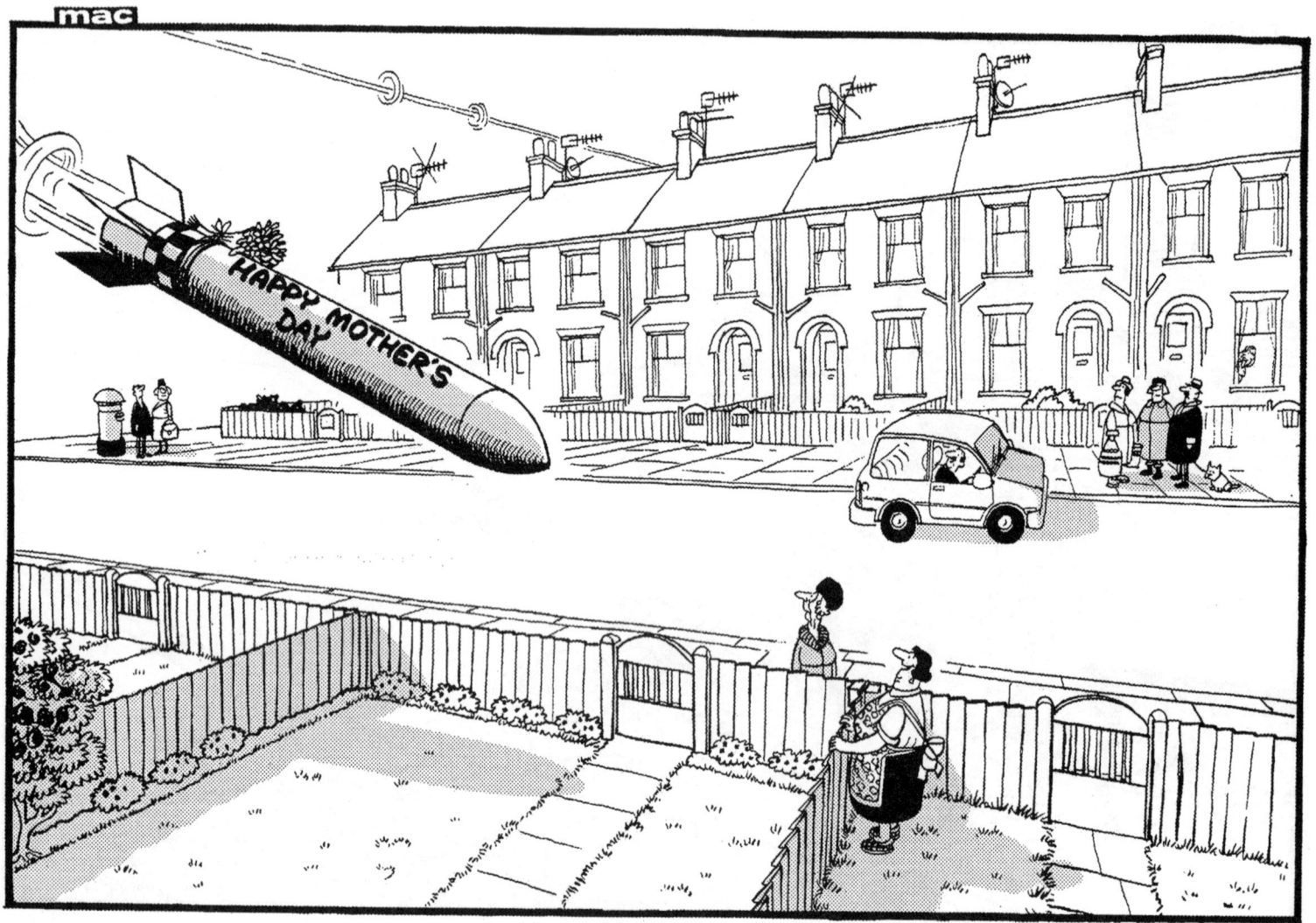

'Aw, bless him. A bit late, but wherever he is he never forgets.' *31 March*

Having resigned with considerable dignity over the war with Iraq, former Leader of the House of Commons Robin Cook lost popular support when he called for British troops to be brought home. He later retracted his statement in a radio interview.

'All together now, when he comes round – April Fool!' *1 April*

The Allied ground assault on Baghdad began after days of relentless aerial bombardment. Meanwhile, Science Minister and supermarket millionaire Lord Sainsbury donated a further £2.5 million to the Labour Party.

'Look. Blair has started the reconstruction already.' *3 April*

As further claims were made by Allied chiefs that Saddam was dead or mortally wounded, more video footage of the Iraqi leader was shown on TV in which he urged his people to fight on and declared that 'victory was at hand'.

'Just stick to: "I'm alive and well, victory is at hand" – cut out that "Gottle o' geer" stuff.' *4 April*

Iraq's second city, Basra, was eventually overrun by Allied troops, but still Saddam's whereabouts were unknown. Though rumoured to have fled the country, new TV film showed him on a walkabout among cheering crowds.

'Right, lads. Another pint then we must go and film another stirring message for our valiant troops back home.' *7 April*

An orgy of looting in the conquered cities of Iraq – including hospitals, museums and government buildings – led to international criticism of the USA for failing to maintain civil law after the collapse of the old regime. But where *was* Saddam?

'Rasheed. This freezer you looted from the palace – guess what?' *11 April*

The launch of the new Saatchi Gallery on London's South Bank included 160 naked men and women who laid down outside the site for a photograph by American artist Spencer Tunick, who specialises in naked crowds around global landmarks.

'Don't think I'm not grateful, Bernard. But a small oil painting for above the mantelpiece would've been lovely.' *17 April*

Easter was marred for more than 100,000 commuters when they were left stranded after rail-union leaders chose the year's busiest rail-travel day to mount a 24-hour strike by train guards.

' 'Arry. All them Easter eggs and hot cross buns what those passengers brought – where did they put them?' *18 April*

A series of advertisements on TV promoted new mobile phones that could take and send pictures. Meanwhile, as millions headed for the coast for the Easter holiday, huge fires swept parts of the countryside after a long period of dry weather.

'This'll cheer them up. That kid who lives next door has sent a photo-text of our house on fire.' *21 April*

There was considerable legal controversy when a surrogate mother from Sunderland decided that she wanted to take back the baby girl she had given birth to, just six days after handing her over to her future parents.

'I just hope his surrogate mother won't mind having him back after all these years.' *22 April*

Labour MP George Galloway was at his luxury home in Portugal when the *Daily Telegraph* published claims that documents discovered in the Iraqi Foreign Ministry in Baghdad suggested he had been paid £375,000 a year by Saddam Hussein.

'**Mr Galloway apologises but he isn't receiving any visitors today.**' *24 April*

An outbreak of more than 300 suspected cases of the deadly SARS (Severe Acute Respiratory Syndrome) virus in Toronto, Canada, led the World Health Organisation to decree it the first Western no-go area. The flu-like virus, which originated in China, is believed to be spread through air travel.

'This is your captain speaking. If anyone else feels a sneeze coming on will they please let the cabin crew know?' *25 April*

The *Sunday Times*'s annual 'Rich List' revealed that 37-year-old J K Rowling, author of the Harry Potter children's books, was Britain's wealthiest self-made woman, with a personal fortune of £280 million, making her richer than the Queen.

'. . . "Aha," cried Harry Windsor, stubbing out his fag and climbing on to his chauffeur-driven broomstick . . .' *28 April*

Six hundred men and women volunteered to pose nude on the escalators in Selfridge's in London's Oxford Street as part of a promotion devoted to body modification and adornment. The event was organised by the American photographer Spencer Tunick.

'Honestly, I felt it as soon as I saw you – you have a tantalising air of mystery about you . . .' *29 April*

Former *EastEnders* actress Danniella Westbrook, who battled for years against cocaine addiction, broke down in tears and asked to leave after only two days in the Australian rainforest as part of ITV's *I'm a Celebrity – Get Me Out of Here!* series.

'Look at him. High as a kite. – He's just swallowed Danniella Westbrook.' *1 May*

The Congestion Charge had been introduced in February to deter motorists from entering central London. Meanwhile, 3,000 demonstrators took to the city's streets in the May Day anti-capitalist march.

'I'm glad you're back from London. There's a bloke here says you forgot to pay the Congestion Charge.' *2 May*

After a week of the new series of ITV's *I'm a Celebrity – Get Me Out of Here!*, hosted by presenters Ant and Dec (Anthony McPartlin and Declan Donnely), TV chef Antony Worrall Thompson led a successful revolt over inadequate food supplies.

'It was a great idea inviting Ant and Dec over for supper. They were delicious.' *6 May*

Shadow Home Secretary Oliver Letwin accused the police of ignoring real crime in favour of easy targets, claiming they preferred issuing parking tickets and arresting speeding motorists to tackling increasing street violence, burglary and drug offences.

'A bit of luck, Sarge. I was just off to caution a harmless, drug-crazed person with a machine-gun when I came across this villain illegally parked.' *9 May*

Scotland Yard mounted an inquiry when it was revealed that a Royal Protection Officer had fired a shot while unloading his gun at Prince Andrew's Berkshire home. Meanwhile, Englishman Paul Casey won the Benson & Hedges Golf Tournament.

'Weird, isn't it? I was just practising with my previous bodyguard when he suddenly stood up, made a funny grunting noise and his gun went off accidentally.' *12 May*

The world's first inflatable church was exhibited at a Christian resources exhibition in Surrey. Made of PVC and designed by Innovations UK, it was 47 feet high, 47 feet long and 25 feet wide, and included a blow-up organ, altar, pulpit and pews.

'Dearly beloved, we are gathered here together on this solemn occasion . . .' *15 May*

Home Secretary David Blunkett attacked a retired High Court Judge as being 'out of touch' when he raised objections to the Government's tough new sentencing guidelines which compelled judges to adopt a 'life means life' policy for murderers.

' "There's no evidence against you," says the judge. "By the way, what d'you think of David Blunkett?" "Nice bloke," I says. "Ten years," he says.' *16 May*

England football captain David Beckham appeared wearing a new hair style, involving tightly plaited braids known as 'cornrows', when he met Liz Hurley and Sir Elton John for lunch in a restaurant near Nice in the south of France.

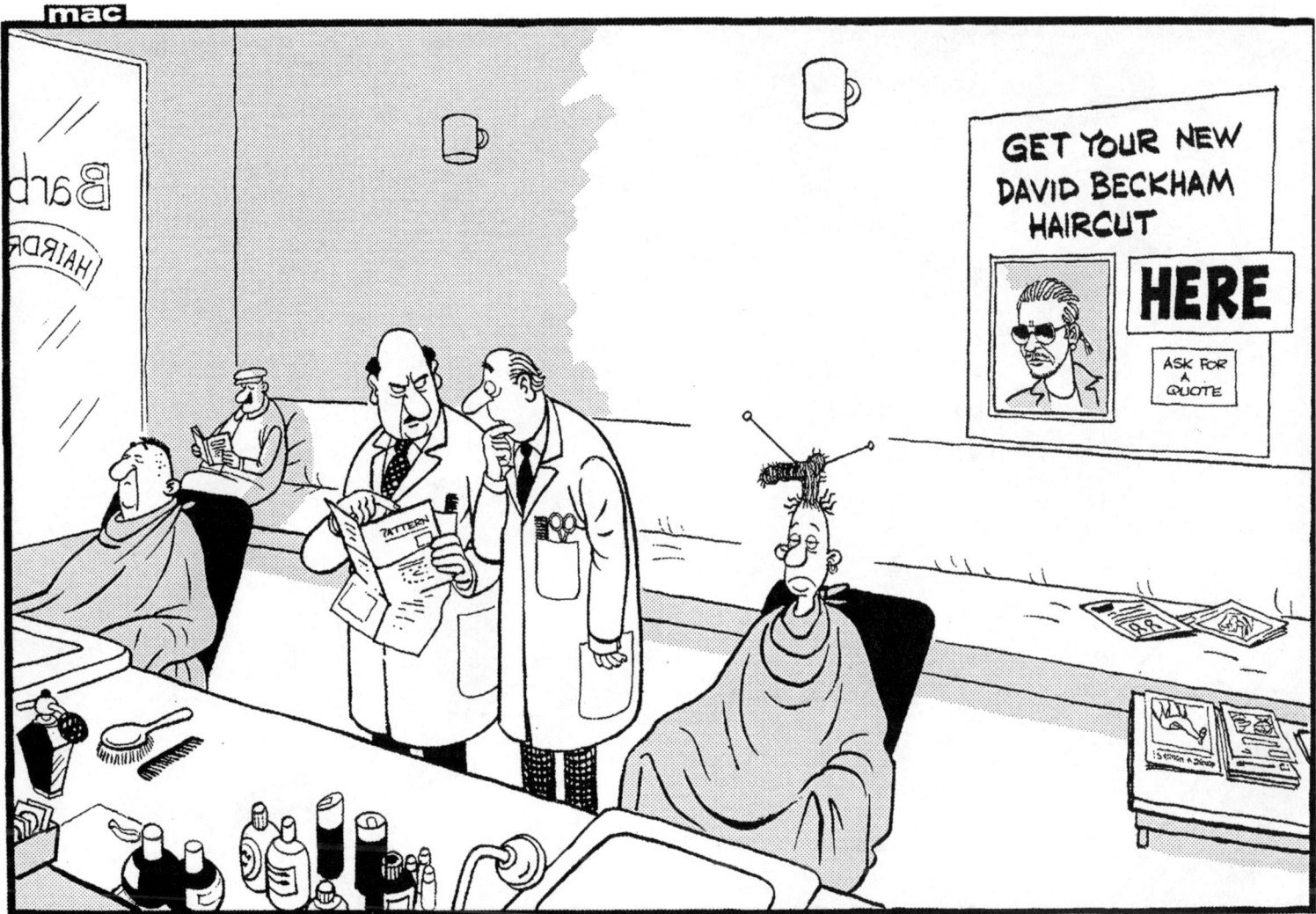

'No, no. It's purl one, plain one, cross-stitch and then cast off – you've knitted a sock.'   *19 May*

There was widespread concern for Britain's sovereignty when the Government announced that there would be no national referendum on a new European constitution drafted by former French President Valery Giscard d'Estaing.

'In its day it was quite an important place, I believe. But the chap in charge handed everything over to new managers in Brussels.' *20 May*

A scientific study based on information gathered by 900 researchers investigating 'ghostly feelings' at famous haunted sites, claimed that these could be explained by environmental factors such as tiny changes in light, temperature, smell and magnetic fields.

'Quiet, please. One question at a time. – You, sir, the man in the third row with his head under his arm . . .' *22 May*

A revolutionary new 'self-parking' car was introduced. The £44,000 BMW X5 Offroader used an onboard computer and ultrasonic sensors to measure the distance between the car, kerb and other vehicles and then automatically steered it into place.

'At only £44,000 it's a bargain. It parks itself, makes a cup of tea and puts 10,000 volts through anyone approaching it with a parking ticket.' *23 May*

Two of Saddam Hussein's three daughters sought asylum in the UK, claiming that as their husbands – both former Saddam aides – had been executed for passing secrets to the West, they would face persecution and even death if they remained in Iraq.

'Look. One is terribly sorry that Blair bombed your palaces, but you're not having this one – now clear orf.' *3 June*

The continued failure to find any evidence of weapons of mass destruction in Iraq led to speculation that the British and US governments had distorted intelligence reports on Saddam's military capability in order to boost public support for the invasion.

'Dad, it's me, Euan. Still no weapons of mass destruction. Only Coke cans and bent nails . . . when can I come home?' *5 June*

There were suggestions that Iraq's chemical and biological weapons had been transferred out of the country. Meanwhile, Saddam Hussein's former wife, Sajida, mother of the dictator's two sons, Uday and Qusay, also applied for asylum in the UK.

'She's got terrible taste. Look at the colour of that settee!' *6 June*

Britain seemed to be moving ever closer to Europe. However, on the issue of the single currency, Chancellor Gordon Brown's long-awaited 1,700-page report – published after six years of study by Treasury experts – concluded 'Not Yet'.

'Nearly there . . . wait for it . . . wait for it . . .'   *10 June*

Millionaire football star David Beckham was taken completely by surprise when he learned that Manchester United's manager, Sir Alex Ferguson, had agreed to sell him to Barcelona for £30 million.

'Spare a thought for Sir Alex Ferguson's wife – I bet she didn't know she was on the market either.' *12 June*

Shortly after the shock resignation of Health Secretary Alan Milburn for 'family reasons', the controversial Lord Chancellor, Lord Irvine, also stood down after negotiating a much-criticised pension deal worth £2.4 million.

13 June

An inquiry was held after a newspaper reporter using bogus references was able to get a job as a guard looking after Ian Huntley – suspected of murdering the schoolgirls Holly Wells and Jessica Chapman – at a top-security prison in Buckinghamshire.

'Careful what you say, Fingers. It could be Lynda Lee-Potter.'   *16 June*

Despite tight security, Aaron Barschak, a self-styled 'comedy terrorist', gatecrashed Prince William's 21st birthday party at Windsor Castle dressed as Osama bin Laden. Meanwhile, the long-awaited new Harry Potter book by J K Rowling was published.

'Complete nutter gatecrashing Prince William's party. Which way please?' *23 June*

As the furore over the breach of royal security at Windsor Castle continued, the Wimbledon tennis tournament began. The Williams sisters, Serena and Venus, from the USA, were both hotly tipped for the women's title.

'Before we start, are you absolutely sure that's Serena Williams?'   *24 June*

As six more British soldiers died in Iraq, there was heated parliamentary debate about who was responsible for the so-called 'dodgy dossier' which the Prime Minister had presented to the House of Commons to justify the attack on Saddam Hussein.

DODGY DOSSIERS *26 June*

'I say! Anyone for f**** tennis?'** *27 June*

The position of Tony Blair's chief spin doctor, Alastair Campbell, seemed to be in jeopardy after allegations were made by a BBC correspondent that he had 'sexed up' intelligence reports in order to get the British public behind the war with Iraq.

'Are you still there? . . . don't go Alastair . . . please, Alastair . . . ALASTAIR!' *30 June*

New plans were unveiled by Deputy Minister for Women and Equality Jacqui Smith to give same-sex couples in long-term relationships the same legal rights – including joint pension rights and 'divorce' settlements – as married couples.

'I'm sorry, Doris. If you and I split up I'll get nothing. But Percy's got a nice pension, a house and his own bike.' *1 July*

Britain's Number One tennis player, Tim Henman, was defeated by Frenchman Sebastien Grosjean in the Wimbledon quarter-finals.

'How did Tim Henman get on?'   *4 July*

The row between Downing Street and the BBC deepened further when the Corporation's Director-General and news chiefs refused to withdraw claims that the Prime Minister and Alastair Campbell had misled Parliament over the Iraqi threat.

'For heaven's sake, Tony! He's only watching *Teletubbies*.' *7 July*

After a meeting with the Archbishop of Canterbury, gay Anglican priest Canon Jeffrey John resigned as Bishop of Reading because of the widespread controversy his appointment had generated in the Christian community.

'What the Church really needs is someone less controversial. Shall I apply, darling?'   *8 July*

In a massive U-turn on transport policy, the Government finally abandoned its anti-car stance and announced a £7 billion road-building programme and nationwide tolls which could see drivers paying up to 50p a mile to travel on Britain's congested roads.

'OK, it's cost us 50p a mile to get here. But smell the air . . . isn't it worth it?'   *10 July*

Tony Blair called a crisis Cabinet meeting after finally admitting that actual evidence of weapons of mass destruction might never be found in Iraq, thereby casting doubt on the main reason for invading the country.

11 July

The 57-year-old former Manchester United football star George Best was involved in a drunken pub brawl in Surrey less than a year after receiving a life-saving liver transplant.

'Just wait till you see this boy dribbling down the field, Sir Alex – I think we've found a new George Best.' *15 July*

As summer temperatures soared to record levels, the Government announced plans to erect thousands of giant 260-foot-high wind turbines off Britain's coastline, in an attempt to reduce greenhouse gases produced by conventional power-stations.

'Oooh. A crab and some pretty shells. What else did you find in the sea?' *16 July*

Former Life Guards officer James Hewitt, who had hit the headlines for trying to sell letters written to him by Princess Diana during their five-year affair, was the subject of a Channel 4 TV documentary, *James Hewitt: Confessions of a Cad.*

'Mind how you go, Mr Hewitt, sir. There's been a sharp increase in violent crime.' *17 July*

Millionaire novelist and former MP Jeffrey Archer was released from prison after serving two years and two days of a four-year sentence for perjury and perverting the course of justice after faking an alibi in a libel case involving the prostitute Monica Coghlan.

'Jeffrey. You're home now! There's no bucket.' *22 July*

Home Secretary David Blunkett revealed plans to use 'restorative justice' schemes – in which criminals apologise to their victims – as an alternative to being prosecuted in court for lesser offences such as minor assaults, car crime and anti-social behaviour.

'Hang on, lads. I'll just make a note of the address so we can write and apologise.' *23 July*

Saddam Hussein's two sons, Uday (aged 39) and Qusay (37), were both killed after a four-hour battle with 200 US troops in Iraq's northern city of Mosul.

'Patience, George, patience! They've only just arrived . . . yes, yes. I'll ask about their dad's weapons of mass destruction . . .'

24 July

The Professional Association of Teachers hit out at Kylie Minogue, Christina Aguilera and other raunchy and scantily dressed female pop stars as being poor role models for young girls, putting them under pressure to grow up too fast and depriving them of their innocence.

'You'll have to excuse Ethel. She's been watching too much Kylie Minogue.' *31 July*

As Britain's immigration problems deepened, 34-year-old Austrian Felix Baumgartner became the first man to fly unaided across the English Channel. With a six-foot wing strapped to his back he jumped from a plane above Dover and glided to France in 12 minutes.

'Remember, Ali. After Calais keep going, then look out for a big open space called Kent.' *1 August*